MW01681340

THE CHEAT CODE

THE CHEAT CODE

UNLOCK THE HIDDEN CODES TO MASTER YOURSELF AND *WIN AT LIFE!*

ARNOLD E. BEST

Real persons and situations have been referenced for demonstrative purposes only, however, their real names have been changed to protect their privacy.

Cover design by Desfia Phillips
Editing and interior layout by Marva Mitchell & Mahaella Mannette
Published by One Momentum Publishing

ISBN 978-1-969564-20-8

Website: www.ompublishing.org

DEDICATION

This book is dedicated to every person who became a mirror, a lesson, or a catalyst in my journey.

To my family: the ones who held me, challenged me, and gave me roots.

To my friends: the ones who walked beside me through seasons of uncertainty and growth.

To my clients: the brave souls who trusted me with their transformation and allowed me to step into my calling with purpose and conviction.

Your faith in me did more than shape my work, it shaped me. You didn't just witness my transformation; you were part of the force that created it.

To the moments that broke me open, the questions that kept me searching, and the curiosity that wouldn't let me settle, thank you. My pain pushed me. My courage carried me. And every chapter of my evolution was forged through these experiences.

Transformation is not a single event; it is a lifetime of becoming.

It is the shedding of old identities, the rewriting of inner stories, and the quiet, persistent decision to rise again and again.

This book exists because I chose to rise.

Because I chose to listen.

Because I chose to transform.

And to the version of myself who walked through the fire so I could stand here today—

I see you.

I honor you.

I am because you endured.

This dedication is for all of us who have been reshaped by life, refined by struggle, and awakened by truth.

May these pages remind you that evolution is your birthright, transformation is your power, and your becoming has only just begun.

■■■

CONTENTS

INTRODUCTION The Moment Everything Changes...1

Chapter 1 DECISION: *The Power to Begin*..................5

Chapter 2 IDENTITY: *Who Are You, Really?*...............15

Chapter 3 OWNERSHIP: *No More Excuses*................22

Chapter 4 THE PURPOSE DROUGHT 28

Chapter 5 BREAKING THE BELIEF CODE....................36

Chapter 6 EMOTIONAL MANAGEMENT....................46

Chapter 7 WHY WE DO WHAT WE DO.....................57

Chapter 8 THE 7 AREAS FOR AN
EXTRAORDINARY LIFE 71

Chapter 9 BE CAREFUL OF YOUR SOURCE 85

Chapter 10 THIS IS THE FASTEST WAY:
To Lose Your Peace 98

Chapter 11 THE ULTIMATE CHANGE CODE 110

Chapter 12 FEAR: *The Illusion That
Steals Your Future*...119

Chapter 13 THE CHEAT CODE EVERYONE
MUST LIVE BY...132

Introduction

The Moment Everything Changes

Every transformation begins with a moment of honesty, that quiet, undeniable whisper that rises above the noise and says, "Your life can be more than this."

For more than a decade, I devoted my life to helping people reconnect with the strongest, clearest, most powerful version of themselves. I spent years coaching, training, speaking, guiding, and walking beside men and women who knew they were meant for more but didn't know how to access it.

I didn't learn this from a distance, I lived it.

My own transformation took me through deep personal work, countless breakthroughs, and one of the most defining experiences of my life–***walking on fire.***

That fire-walk wasn't a stunt.

It wasn't a hype moment.

It was a reminder that the limits we fear are often nothing more than illusions we've mistakenly accepted as truth. I understood that human change isn't complicated, ***it's coded.***

If you understand the code, you can change your life.

If you don't, you keep repeating the same patterns and calling it fate.

This book holds the codes.

These pages won't just teach you how to change. They'll teach you how to take ownership, how to shift your identity, how to break belief patterns, master your emotions, and align your life with a version of you that's been waiting beneath the surface.

You'll find clarity.

You'll find a challenge.

You'll find conviction.

And most importantly, you'll ***find yourself.***

Inside these chapters are the same principles I've used on myself, on clients across the world, on teams, executives, parents, dreamers, and everyday people who finally said, ***'I'm ready'.***

If you're holding this book, I believe it's because something in you is ready to step into the next version of who you are.

Not the version shaped by doubt, history, or fear, but the version shaped by truth, clarity, purpose, and power.

Identity. Ownership. Purpose.

Chapter 1
DECISION: *The Power to Begin*

'Your life doesn't move in the direction of your intentions; it moves in the direction of your decisions.'

For seven years, one of my clients worked in a 'good government job', the kind of job people fight for, pray for, and never leave. He had the benefits. He had stability. He had a pension. He had the respect of family who said, "Boy, hold on to that. Yuh set for life". But every morning, the closer he got to the building he worked in, the more his chest tightened.

He told me, there were days he drove around the block twice, pretending to look for parking just so he could delay stepping inside. He wasn't lazy. He wasn't lost. He was quietly dying inside a life that looked 'successful' but didn't feel like his. One Monday morning in particular changed everything.

He woke up before his alarm, not because he was ready, but because his mind wouldn't let him rest. He showered, dressed, ironed his shirt crisp like always, and left the house before the sun fully rose. But when he reached downtown, he didn't go inside. He sat in his car. Engine on. Radio off. Hands gripping the steering wheel.

He watched people walking into the same building he should have been entering, some smiling, some rushing, some looking just as drained as he felt. He said the pressure in his chest started to build until it felt like his whole body was vibrating. He couldn't breathe properly. He felt like his mind was whispering, "You can't keep living like this."

He placed his head on the steering wheel and whispered something he had never admitted to himself before, "This job is killing my spirit." He didn't care about the pension at that moment. He didn't care about the title. He didn't care about what family or friends would say. For the first time, he saw the truth in raw daylight.

He had built his entire life on what everyone else expected of him and not a single decision came from his own soul. He sat in that car for almost forty minutes. And inside that silence, something shifted. Not loudly. Not dramatically. But with finality.

He decided that he would no longer trade his peace for a pay-check.

He decided that his life would not be defined by a job description.

He decided that he would no longer carry pride in something that brought him misery.

He decided that he was worth more than survival.

He didn't walk into the HR office that day and resign.

But he walked inside knowing he would not be there forever.

And that single decision, made alone in a parked car on a Monday morning in the heart of Port of Spain, set off a chain reaction in his entire life. He started studying in the evenings for something he actually cared about. He began saving intentionally for the first time. He slowly detached his identity from the title he carried.

He prepared quietly, patiently, strategically.

When the day came for him to submit his resignation, he told me he felt something he hadn't felt in years; lightness. His family didn't understand at first. Some friends laughed. Some coworkers said he was 'brave' while others said he was 'mad'.

But he kept moving.

Today, he wakes up at 4:30a.m. not because he has to but because he wants to. He has built a life that gives him purpose instead of panic. Peace instead of pressure. Ownership instead of obligation. And every time he drives through Port of Spain, he passes by the building he used to fear entering and smiles; not because he escaped it, but because inside that parked car on a Monday morning, he finally made a decision that belonged to him.

You don't need more time. You need to decide.

Because time doesn't make you ready, decisions do. Let's get real.

Most people are stuck, not because they don't know what to do, but because they won't **DECIDE** to do it.

They're waiting for the right feeling. Waiting for a sign. Waiting for fear to disappear. But here's the code; fear leaves the moment a decision enters.

Every breakthrough, every shift, every transformation you admire started with a moment. One decision. A line in the sand. A 'no more'. A 'never again'. A 'from now on'.

That moment you say:

"I'm done tolerating this."

"I choose a new standard."

"I decide to move, even if I don't have it all figured out."

Because life meets you at the level of your decision. Not your potential. Not your talent.

Not your dreams. But at your decision.

DISCOVERY AND TRANSFORMATION

Reset Point:

'Take Back Your Control.'

- ☐ ***What have I been postponing?***
- ☐ ***What have I been circling with excuses and overthinking?***
- ☐ ***Where have I allowed doubt to take control of my destiny.***

When you decide, you collapse time. You activate the part of you that's been waiting. The power isn't in the plan, it's in the pivot.

SECRET LEVEL:

- ☐ ***What truth have I been avoiding because I didn't want to decide?***
- ☐ ***What pain am I prolonging by staying in limbo?***
- ☐ ***What's ONE decision I can make today, that changes everything?***

Check Point:

"I'm No Longer Available For…"

Write a list of things you're no longer available for. Old patterns, excuses, environments, and stories.

Choose **ONE** and decide, this ends now.

____

____

____

____

____

____

____

____

Speak it. Feel it. Live it. Decision isn't just a moment. It's a message to the world.

I AM READY NOW!

Learn To Burn Your Boats

There comes a point in every journey, where turning back isn't just impossible–it's unacceptable. That's what 'burning your boats' really means. It's the moment you look at where you came from, you look at where you're going, and you realise the past can't be your escape plan anymore. No more safety nets. No more 'if it doesn't work, I'll just go back'.

NO MORE!

The story of 'burning your boats' comes from an army that landed on enemy shores. The commander looked at his men, tired, unsure, already thinking about retreat and gave one order: "*Burn the boats!*"

At first the soldiers panicked. *"How will we get home?"*

He said, *"We either win…or we die here."*

That single **decision** changed everything.

Their fear turned into focus.

Their uncertainty turned into commitment.

Their excuses disappeared because there was nowhere left to run.

And they won.

That's what it feels like when you finally get tired of half-stepping in your own life. When you stop entertaining your old patterns. When you close doors that were never meant to stay open. When you strip away the fallback options that keep you trapped in the same version of yourself.

Burning your boats isn't reckless.

It's declaring to life: "I'm all in. And the only direction from here is forward."

And the moment you do that, something powerful happens.

Your energy shifts.

Your identity strengthens.

And the universe moves things that were never available to you when you were still negotiating with your fears.

Sometimes the breakthrough isn't in doing more. It's just stepping a bit out of your **comfort zone.**

Commitment doesn't start with energy.

It starts with a vow. A line you draw that says, **'Even when it's hard, I'm still in'.**

Most people flirt with their goals. But flirting won't build your future. Commitment will. You don't need another motivational speech; you need to burn those boats of comfort.

No plan B.

No backup exit.

You go all in. Because halfway energy gets halfway results.

This is what commitment sounds like:

☑ ***"I will finish what I start."***

☑ ***"I'm not here to try; I'm here to transform."***

☑ ***"This is not a hobby. This is who I am."***

And when you commit, you'll notice something powerful–the world starts moving around your decision. Resources show up. Opportunities open. Why?

Because you moved first.

DISCOVERY AND TRANSFORMATION

SECRET LEVEL:

- ☐ ***Where in my life have I been half in?***
- ☐ ***What am I treating as optional that needs to become non-negotiable?***
- ☐ ***When I am fully committed, what would I do differently?***

Check Point:

'The No-Matter-What List'

Make a list of **THREE things** you will commit to, no matter what.

____

____

____

____

____

____

These are your promises to yourself.

Keep them sacred.

Keep them strong.

Commitment is a choice you make daily. Not just once. Not just when it's easy. You commit. **Every. Single. Day.**

■■■

Chapter 2
IDENTITY: *Who Are You, Really?*

'You will never outperform and out decide the version of yourself you believe or decide you are.'

Identity is the unseen engine behind everything you do. It quietly determines what you try, what you avoid, what you tolerate, and what you believe is possible for you. Most people don't fail because of lack of talent or desire, they fail because they are *living from an identity that can't carry the life they want.*

One of my clients grew up in a family where expectations were louder than dreams. From young, she was the one everybody depended on, the one who got good grades, kept the house steady, handled responsibilities before she even understood what childhood was supposed to feel like. By the time she reached her twenties, she wasn't living her life, she was performing the identity her family gave her. She became the dependable daughter. The steady sister. The **'don't-worry-I'll-handle-it'** person.

Her life looked safe from the outside, but inside she felt like she was disappearing.

Her real passion was photography, something she hid like a guilty pleasure. In the evenings she'd sit on her back step and watch how the sunset hit the old coconut trees behind her house. She would imagine capturing it, framing it, turning it into art. But every time the urge to pursue it grew strong, she heard the same messages she grew up on:

"Art can't pay bills."

"You need a real job."

"Yuh want to take pictures for your whole life?"

"You're a dreamer."

Those weren't just comments, those were identities being placed on her, identities she felt obligated to wear. She convinced herself to stay small because she didn't want to disappoint the people she loved. She stayed in a job that drained her, surrounded by people who told her to be **'grateful'** because she had stability. But stability without authenticity feels like a prison.

Her breaking point came the day she realized she was waking up every morning with a heaviness she could not explain. Not sadness. Something worse, what we called, ***'unlived potential'.***

We started working together, and during one session, she paused, looked down at her hands, and whispered, ***"All my life I am living who they want me to be, I don't even know who I am."***

That was the moment her identity cracked open; her first step wasn't quitting her job. It wasn't buying an expensive camera. It wasn't launching a business. Her first step was giving herself permission to want what she truly wanted. She started posting a few photos–sunsets, people in the market, her niece playing in the yard. People loved them. She booked her first small shoot for a friend. Then another, then a paid one. Word spread fast because her photos didn't just capture faces, they captured souls.

Within months, she built a steady side income. Within a year, she surpassed what she earned from her ***'safe'*** job. Today, her clients range from families to local entrepreneurs. But the real transformation wasn't financial, it was internal. She stopped being the responsible girl everyone depended on. She stopped being the quiet daughter who stayed inside the lines.

She stopped being the woman who lived under the weight of other people's expectations.

She stepped into a new identity, one she chose, one she earned, one she finally recognized as her own. Her life changed the moment she stopped carrying the labels others gave her and started claiming the name she always had–***Artist.***

You see, your results will never outgrow your identity.

You can change habits, routines, systems, environments, even relationships, but if the identity beneath it all remains the same, the results will snap back to match it. That's why people who ***'start over'*** often end up right back where they began. The identity didn't shift, only the false behaviour did.

Every habit you repeat. Every standard you set. Every boundary you enforce or ignore. Every dream you pursue or abandon, is shaped by the *story* you tell yourself about who you are.

When you say things like: 'I'm not disciplined', 'I'm not confident', 'That's just not me', you're not describing your truth; you're describing your *limiting belief.*

You're not labelling your personality; you're limiting your potential. Identity is the internal script that determines how far you're allowed to go. And most people are living their lives trapped inside an outdated script.

Some identities were shaped by ***survival.***

Some were shaped by someone else's ***expectations.***

Some were shaped by ***fear, failure, or a moment you never healed from.***

But none of those identities define who you really are.

The deeper work isn't about becoming someone new. It is about peeling back everything you picked up along the way–the fear, the performance, the pressure–and remembering the version of you that existed before you started shrinking. Change the ***meaning,*** and you change the life attached to it. This isn't about pretending. It's about returning; returning to the truest, boldest, most aligned version of you.

DISCOVERY AND TRANSFORMATION

RESET POINT:

Who am I becoming?

And who must I stop being to meet them?

When you stop defending the outdated identity, you make room for the identity that can carry your vision. You step into the version of you that leads with clarity instead of insecurity, intention instead of fear, and purpose instead of pressure.

'Stop trying to change your life while protecting the identity that's limiting it.'

SECRET LEVEL:

- ☐ ***What identity have I been dragging that no longer fits the life I'm asking for?***
- ☐ ***What version of me am I protecting that is secretly holding me back?***
- ☐ ***If I fully trusted who I truly am, what would I stop settling for?***
- ☐ ***Where am I still acting like the old me, even though the new me is ready to take the lead?***
- ☐ ***What identity must I lay to rest so the real me can rise?***
- ☐ ***Don't rush these. Identity speaks when your spirit gets quiet.***

CHECK POINT:

'I Am Becoming'

This exercise isn't imagination, it's instruction.

Write a letter from your future self, the one who already made the identity shift. This identity becomes the blueprint for your next step. Borrow their voice. Borrow their posture. Borrow their clarity.

They are you without the fear, without the noise, without the labels you've outgrown.

Let this version describe:

- ☑ How you'll think under pressure.
- ☑ How you'll speak to yourself.
- ☑ How you'll walk into rooms.
- ☑ What you no longer tolerate.
- ☑ What you allow yourself to receive.
- ☑ How you love, lead, work, decide, and show up.

Identity isn't discovered, identity is chosen.

And today, **YOU CHOOSE!**

■■■

Chapter 3
OWNERSHIP: *No More Excuses*

'The moment you take ownership of your life, excuses lose their power.'

Excuses are the most expensive stories you'll ever tell yourself. They drain your time, your confidence, and the power you need to create the life you keep imagining. Every time you blame something or someone, you hand your future to an outside force. Every time you take ownership, you take back your future.

I worked with a teacher from Arima, a while back in my career. She had a heart so big it seemed to hold everyone around her–her students, her colleagues, her family, even strangers, she carried them all. For years, she believed giving everything was the right thing to do. She stayed late grading papers, stayed even later helping students with personal problems, and brought work home every night. She lent money, offered advice, cooked for her extended family, and always said "yes", even when she wanted to say no.

On the outside, everyone called her selfless, dedicated, and dependable. On the inside, she was silently breaking. She began to notice the cracks in subtle ways; a tension in her shoulders that never left, a fatigue that sleep could not fix, a constant sense of being ***'on duty'*** that followed her everywhere. She was giving her energy, her time, her life, yet she felt emptier than ever.

For years, she told herself the same lie, ***"I'm doing this for them. I'm responsible for them. They need me."*** She did not realize the truth until one day she fainted at work. When she woke up in the hospital, the doctor shook his head and said, ***"Miss, you're running on empty."***

It hit her like a thunderbolt. All these years she had blamed the system, the workload, the stress, but the real problem was that she never took ownership of her own life.

She had been giving without boundaries, without self-respect, without claiming responsibility for her own energy and well-being. That realization was painful, but it was also freeing. She began to make small, intentional changes. She blocked twenty minutes every morning just for herself, to meditate, stretch, or breathe. She learned to say 'no' without guilt, realizing that refusing wasn't selfish; it was necessary.

She started asking for support, delegating, and letting others take responsibility instead of shouldering everything alone. She refused to let other people's needs define her emotional state. At first, it was hard. Students, colleagues, even family questioned her boundaries.

"Why are you being so strict with your time?" they asked. Her answer was simple, ***"Because I finally decided my life matters, too."***

Slowly, her energy returned. Her patience returned. Her joy returned. She could still give, but now she gave from fullness instead of emptiness. Ownership didn't mean she gave less. It meant she was no longer giving blindly. It meant she was taking responsibility for her life first, and only then sharing what she could freely give. By reclaiming her energy, she transformed everything; her work, her family, her health, and even the way people responded to her. She learned the hardest, most important lesson. You cannot pour from an empty cup.

And the first step to changing your life is taking full ownership of it.

Most people never grow because they're still loyal to their limitations. They defend patterns that are holding them hostage. They explain why they can't instead of deciding how they will. They stay waiting for conditions to improve instead of improving their approach. And at the root of almost every excuse is one thing; a low ***standard*** you've been tolerating.

When you raise ***your standards,*** excuses lose their room to live. You stop negotiating with your potential. You stop accepting behaviours, environments, and habits that don't match the future you want. You stop settling for old levels of *effort, discipline, and self-respect.*

Raising your standards is the real turning point.

It's the moment you say:

- ☑ ***"Taking my 'Shoulds' and making it a 'Must'."***
- ☑ ***"This is no longer acceptable."***
- ☑ ***"This version of me is expired."***
- ☑ ***"I'm done explaining my limitations."***

Ownership demands honesty. The kind that might create pain for a moment, but frees you for a lifetime.

It asks:

- ☐ ***What area in my life am I choosing comfort over growth?***
- ☐ ***What have I been blaming instead of facing?***
- ☐ ***What standards have I allowed to slip?***
- ☐ ***What am I tolerating that is not serving me and allowing me to shut down immediately?***

Your life rises, or falls, to the level of your standards. Raise them, and your behaviour automatically follows. Raise them high enough, and excuses can't breathe.

Taking ownership doesn't mean you control every event. It means you control your response, and your response determines your trajectory. When you lead your life by taking ownership of it instead of reacting to it, everything; ***your identity, performance, relationships, and opportunities,*** moves upward.

The truth is simple:

Your results will not change until your standards change.

Your standards will not change until you take full ownership.

Everything you want; greater clarity, income, peace, confidence, purpose, demands that moment where you stop explaining your life and start directing it.

Ownership is that moment.

Raising your standards is what locks it in.

'You can't live an extraordinary life while accepting ordinary standards.'

SECRET LEVEL:

- ☐ Identify three areas where your standards have slipped.
- ☐ Write the new standard you're choosing from this moment forward.
- ☐ Name the excuse that has been protecting the old standard.
- ☐ Replace it with one action you will take in the next 24 hours.
- ☐ Declare out loud: "I raise my standards. I own my life."

■■■

Chapter 4

The Purpose Drought

'A lack of purpose doesn't empty your calendar, it drains your spirit.'

There comes a moment in every high-achiever's life where the grind becomes dry. You're waking up early. Checking boxes. Running the business. Showing up for everyone. But something's off.

It's not burnout. You've been burned out before. This is different. This is a drought. A Purpose Drought. And this drought doesn't care how good your systems are, how strong your resume looks, or how many zeros you see in your account. **IT DOESN'T!**

It whispers louder the more you try to ignore it:

"Why am I doing all this?"

"Who am I doing it for?"

"Does this even matter?"

And for the first time in a long time. You don't have the answers. This is a sign you're in a ***drought.***

One client from Tobago, had spent most of his twenties hustling. He worked two, sometimes three jobs; delivery, construction, even helping neighbours with odd jobs, just to make ends meet and support his family. On the outside, he looked like a hardworking young man everyone admired. But inside, he felt a constant, gnawing emptiness.

No matter how much money he earned, how many hours he put in, or how many people praised him, he could not shake the sense that something was missing. One weekend he flew me over to Tobago for a session. He met me in the late afternoon, shoulders slumped, eyes tired.

He said to me, "I work myself to the bone, but I wake up every day feeling like nothing's really mine. I don't know who I'm working for anymore." He couldn't put it into words, but I could see it, the drought. The lack of purpose had quietly eaten away at his soul.

That afternoon after our first session, I gave him a lot to think about and he went for a walk along the beach to clear his head. The sun was low, painting the horizon gold. Fishermen were hauling in their catch, their movements steady, deliberate, and rhythmic. They weren't rich. They didn't have flashy cars or big houses. But there was something alive in the way they worked, a connection to their craft, their community, ***their purpose.***

And that was when something sank in him. He realized he had spent years chasing money and survival, but not meaning. The work itself wasn't bringing fulfilment; it was only keeping him alive. He had been surviving instead of living. The next day, in our second session we created a Massive Action Plan (M.A.P). He decided to take a re-look of a skill he had loved since childhood, which was woodworking. Over the weeks, he started small, crafting stools, chairs, and tables in a tiny corner of his house. At first, it was just a hobby, a way to feel alive again.

But the more he worked with his hands, shaping raw wood into something tangible, the more he felt connected to life. Each piece reminded him that he could create something that mattered. Something that carried his imprint. Something that was his. It wasn't easy. Family and friends questioned him. "Why waste time with this? You're already *wukking*, boy. You have stability," they said. And he ignored them.

He started selling small pieces locally; neighbours, friends, even the occasional tourist. Slowly, the orders grew. Soon, his craft wasn't just therapy, it became a sustainable source of income.

But the real transformation for him was the soul shift. For the first time in years, he woke up with energy. He went to sleep feeling satisfied. He no longer felt like a passenger in his own life. He was the creator. The maker. The one who decided what mattered.

That young man learned one of the most important lessons during our sessions. That survival without purpose is exhausting. Purpose, no matter how small, brings life back to the soul.

And in the quiet hum of a workshop in Tobago, he finally found the fulfilment he had been chasing for years.

Your 'Purpose Drought' doesn't hit like a storm. It creeps in slowly. It is the moment your wins start to feel like tasks. It's success that no longer excites you. It's passion turning into performance. It is you, giving everything, but getting nothing back in return. You look successful on paper. But inside, you're dehydrated or even empty.

Your soul thirsts for something deeper; not just goals. But meaning. We've been taught to keep going. ***'Power through.' 'Push harder.' 'Winners never quit.' Yeah, right!***

Listen to me, sometimes the most powerful move is not to push, but to pause. Because, a goal without purpose is just ***glorified survival.*** You were not designed to live in constant output. You were built for ***alignment (And alignment is The Structure of Purpose).*** But if you never stop long enough to ask, "Is this still the direction I'm meant to go?" You'll perform your way into emptiness.

I have been there on many occasions, but when that quiet voice inside, says "It's not time to add more to your plate." It's time to listen. Purpose speaks softly. It shows up in discomfort. In dissatisfaction. In the pull toward something more real, more you. You won't find it in applause. You won't find it in promotions. You'll find it in the quiet. That place where ego shuts up and truth speaks.

You see, purpose isn't always about what you do. It's about who you are, when no one is watching (your identity). It's the sacred fire inside you that refuses to be silenced; we call it *HUNGER*. It is not something you choose. It is something that chooses you. And the longer you ignore it, the heavier life feels. You're working, but not fulfilled. Moving, but not arriving. Busy, but not becoming. Many are living full schedules and empty lives. Running fast…but in the wrong direction. Because success without purpose is just a *polished prison;* looks good on the outside, feels hollow on the inside.

But here's the truth: You were born for something bigger than comfort. You were designed to build, to impact, to shift atmospheres. Purpose isn't passive. It's not pretty. It will break your routines, confront your fears, stretch your identity. But in that stretching, it will reveal the version of you you've always been destined to become. When you step into purpose, your life begins to speak without saying a word.

You become magnetic. Not because you're trying to impress, but because you're living in alignment. *And alignment is attractive.* When you walk on purpose, peace follows you. Prosperity and provision find you. People recognize you, not the brand version, not the performing version, but the real, raw, **powerful YOU.**

Purpose brings clarity. It brings conviction. It makes it easier to say no to distractions because you finally know what deserves your 'yes'. And once you've tasted it, you can't go back to the ordinary or average. Because ordinary and average becomes offensive to a soul that's tasted destiny.

DISCOVERY AND TRANSFORMATION

RESET POINT:

- ☐ ***What truly matters to me right now?***
- ☐ ***What do I want my life to mean?***
- ☐ ***Who am I trying to impress... and why?***

Then, you make the scary decision to stop chasing what drains you and start walking toward what ignites you. Yes, it will cost you.

But not as much as not living for our purpose.

CHECK POINT:

"If it Doesn't Align with My Soul, I'm Allowed to Walk Away."

Not everything that fits your schedule fits your spirit.

- ☑ ***If it dehydrates your joy, leave it.***
- ☑ ***If it doesn't light you up, question it.***
- ☑ ***If it demands your time but steals your peace, release it.***

This life is too sacred to spend stuck in performance while your purpose dries up behind the scenes.

There comes a point in every life where the noise gets too loud and the applause too empty. You've climbed the ladder, checked the boxes, smiled for the cameras, but deep inside…something still feels missing.

That emptiness. That quiet ache beneath the surface.

That's purpose calling.

SECRET LEVEL:

Step Into Your Purpose

Take a deep breath. Go within. Now ask yourself:

1. ***Where in my life am I succeeding outwardly but starving inwardly?***

2. ***What makes me feel most alive, even if it scares me?***

3. ***What am I constantly drawn to that I've been ignoring?***

4. ***If I weren't afraid of failing, what would I start doing today?***

5. ***Where have I traded purpose for comfort, and what am I willing to reclaim?***

You weren't born to blend in. You weren't created to just survive. You were designed to lead, to awaken, to rebuild what others gave up on. Your purpose is not random. It is assigned. You're just overdue for a realignment. And this world needs the full version of you. No more delay. No more pretending. The time is now. The fire is yours. ***Live it!***

■■■

Chapter 5
BREAKING THE BELIEF CODE

'Most limits aren't real, they're inherited stories repeated long enough to feel true.'

Your life is 'perfectly designed' to give you the results you are getting right now. Not because you aren't capable. Not because you don't have potential. But because the beliefs running your mind have been quietly running your life. Most people never question the *'belief code'* they were programmed with. They just live inside it, defending it, protecting it, and repeating it. The tragedy is this, *you're fighting battles your beliefs created.*

In the Caribbean most people grew up hearing the same messages over and over: "You have to work twice as hard to be noticed", "You can't make mistakes", "You have to prove yourself constantly". By the time they have reached adulthood, those words become their internal narrative.

They believed, deep down, that they weren't enough. Not smart enough. Not capable enough. Not deserving enough.

Every decision made was filtered through that belief. At work, you stayed quiet during meetings, afraid your ideas would be dismissed. At home, you overextended yourself, always trying to please, never asking for what you needed. In your friendships, you gave more than you received, constantly worrying that asserting yourself would push people away.

Years passed and you built a respectable career, earned recognition, and maintained strong relationships, but you never felt fulfilled. There was always a quiet, gnawing doubt: "I'm not really enough. One day they'll see that too."

This happened to a couple of people I worked with, and in the case of one particular client, the breaking point came when she was overlooked for a promotion she deserved. It felt like validation for the story she had carried her whole life. She questioned herself, "Maybe they're right. Maybe I'm not enough."

When I began working with her, we began uncovering the origins of that belief. We explored every moment where she had internalized it, from childhood criticisms to societal expectations to subtle messages from family and peers. She realized that the story she had believed for decades wasn't true; it was inherited, repeated, and went unchallenged.

The transformation began with small, deliberate actions I encouraged her to use. I also introduced her to her archetypes and how and when to use them. She started speaking up in meetings, sharing ideas even if they felt risky. She said 'no' to extra tasks she didn't want to do, realizing setting boundaries wasn't selfish. She actively celebrated her achievements instead of downplaying them. She experimented with new projects, taking ownership of her creativity without waiting for permission or approval. At first, the change felt uncomfortable. Doubts and old narratives still surfaced. But with each step, she grew stronger. Slowly, she felt the belief that had once paralyzed her begin to crumble.

Within months, she stepped into leadership roles she had previously thought were out of reach. She earned respect not only for her work but for her confidence and authenticity. She began mentoring others who struggled with the same internal barriers she had carried. Most importantly, she finally felt she was enough, one of the most powerful lessons she had working with me. She had ***rewritten*** the story for herself.

Beliefs are not facts. They are stories we tell ourselves. And the moment we challenge them, we reclaim our power.

Yes, your belief code is the invisible script that decides your ceiling, your reactions, your standards, and even what you think you deserve. And until you break that code, nothing changes.

The Invisible Prison:

Limiting beliefs do not show up as loud voices. They show up as patterns.

- ☑ ***Procrastination is a belief.***
- ☑ ***Self-doubt is a belief.***
- ☑ ***Settling is a belief.***
- ☑ ***Avoiding discomfort is a belief.***
- ☑ ***Feeling 'not ready' is a belief.***

Every time you shrink yourself, hesitate, or sabotage your own growth, it's not because you're weak; it's because a belief is telling you that who you are is not equal to what you want.

Limiting beliefs are dangerous because they hide in your *identity.* They feel like the truth, but they are nothing more than repeated thoughts that became emotional habits.

Every Belief You Hold Came from One of Three Places:

1. Someone you trusted: *A parent, teacher, partner, pastor, coach; someone whose voice carried weight. Their words became your internal dialogue.*

2. An emotional moment: *A painful experience. A failure. A disappointment. A rejection. Your nervous system made meaning out of a moment, and that meaning became a rule.*

3. Repetition: *A lie repeated enough times becomes a belief. A belief repeated enough becomes an identity. An identity repeated enough becomes a lifestyle. And that lifestyle becomes your destiny, unless you interrupt it.*

The Belief Code Always Shows Its Hand

If you ever want to know your belief code, don't check your potential, check your patterns.

- ☐ ***What do you settle for?***
- ☐ ***Where do you hesitate most?***
- ☐ ***Who do you keep attracting?***
- ☐ ***What do you avoid facing?***
- ☐ ***Where do you make excuses?***

People don't attract what they want, they attract what they believe they deserve.

The Three Most Common Limiting Beliefs

1. **I'm not enough, and I won't be loved.** This is the root of almost everything:
    - Not smart enough
    - Not talented enough
    - Not loved enough
    - Not worthy

    This belief keeps people performing instead of becoming, pleasing instead of expressing, settling instead of rising.

2. **Good things aren't for people like me.** People carry family stories, generational patterns, and cultural narratives as if they are destiny.

3. **If I try and fail, it will prove I'm not capable.** This belief keeps people living safe, predictable lives. Staying small feels safer than being exposed. But safety kills destiny.

The Shift:

You can't break a belief with motivation. You break it by challenging it, replacing it, and proving it wrong with new experiences.

RESET POINT:

Step 1: Identify the Old Belief

Ask yourself: What belief is keeping me here? **Name it. Expose it. Bring it into the light.**

____

____

____

____

Step 2: Challenge the belief

A belief that is questioned loses its power. Ask: Who taught me this? Were they even qualified to write my narrative?

____

____

____

____

Step 3: Replace the belief

Create a new belief aligned with your identity shift. Not just a positive statement, an upgraded truth.

Example:

OLD: "I'm not enough."

NEW: "I rise every time I show up."

Step 4: Condition the new belief

Beliefs do not change by saying them. They change by reinforcing it. Your actions must be repeated until the nervous system accepts it as truth.

Step 5: Reinforce it through standards

Your standards are the guardians of your new belief. When you raise your standards, your new beliefs will thrive. When you lower your standards, your old beliefs will thrive.

The Identity Link

Your beliefs are the foundation of your identity.

If you believe you are broken, you will sabotage success. If you believe you're behind, you'll force yourself into burnout. If you believe you're unworthy, you'll tolerate disrespect.

But when you believe you are capable, chosen, guided, and equipped, your entire life reorganizes itself around that identity.

Changing your beliefs isn't mindset work. It's identity reconstruction. There comes a moment in your transformation when you realize this: Your old life wasn't holding you back, your old beliefs were. The day you decide that your past no longer has authority over your future…that's the day you break the limiting belief code. From that moment, you don't live from memory, you live from vision. You stop repeating old patterns, you create new ones.

You stop surviving, you evolve.

SECRET LEVEL:

Rewrite Your Code

1. Identify one limiting belief that has shaped your decisions.

2. Write where it came from.

3. Write how it has cost you, emotionally, financially, relationally and spiritually.

4. Write the upgraded belief you are choosing today.

5. Take one small action today that aligns with the new belief.

This is not journaling. This is reprogramming.

■■■

Chapter 6

EMOTIONAL MANAGEMENT

'Emotions are signals, not commands.
Master them, and you master your life.'

There is a moment in every person's life when they realize that the battles they've been fighting were never against the world...they were against themselves. Your real arena is not *'out there'*. It's the space between your ears and behind your ribs (heart and mind). Mastering your emotions isn't optional. It's the *foundation* of every victory, every breakthrough, every transformation.

Nothing in your life improves until your inner world does. You see, two people can live the same moment and walk away with two different destinies. One empowered, one defeated, all because of the meaning they attach to the experience. Once you understand that, you stop being a passenger in your life.

I worked with someone, who had spent most of her life feeling like anxiety was her constant companion. It did not matter whether it was a minor disagreement at work, an unexpected phone call, or simply leaving the house, her mind would spiral into panic and stress.

She believed that her emotions were uncontrollable; that anxiety was something she just had to live with. Every day felt like walking on a tightrope, one misstep, and everything could unravel. She avoided social gatherings, never spoke up in meetings, and rarely pursued opportunities because her mind had already decided she would fail.

"I feel like I'm always waiting for the other shoe to drop," she told me one day. "Even small things feel like disasters waiting to happen. I can't breathe sometimes, and I don't know how to stop it."

Her anxiety wasn't just a mental burden, it affected her body too–sleepless nights, tight shoulders, racing heart, shallow breaths. She felt trapped inside her own life.

We began working on reframing how she saw emotions. She learned that emotions are not dictators, they are signals; action signals to be exact. Signals that point out something that needs attention, but they do not have to control behaviour.

Step by step, she learned to re-name the emotion; ***'I am feeling anxious.'*** Understand it, ***'This is my fear of being judged.'***

She responded consciously, instead of reacting automatically. She took a deep breath, grounded herself, and chose a deliberate action. She also incorporated journaling to process her thoughts, meditation and Neurolinguistic Programming (NLP) to calm her nervous system, and set small challenges to face anxiety head on, like speaking up in a meeting or attending a social event for just ten minutes.

At first, it was uncomfortable. Her mind resisted. Old habits of avoidance tried to pull her back. But every time she practiced and anchored herself, she proved to herself that she could handle the discomfort without it controlling her.

I taught her the art of transformational vocabulary; how a single shift in the words she used could redirect her entire emotional state. She began to see that language isn't just expression; it's a steering wheel. The moment she interrupted the harsh, heavy labels she placed on her experiences, her nervous system softened, her mind opened, and her decisions became clearer. Changing 'I'm overwhelmed' to 'I'm adjusting', or 'This is too much' to 'This is a challenge I can handle', altered the emotional patterns that once controlled her actions. With each new word, she reclaimed authority over her inner world, proving that transformation often begins with the simplest tool we overlook–our vocabulary.

Within a couple of weeks, the difference was remarkable. She no longer avoided life. She could engage fully in her work, pursue opportunities she had once feared, and enjoy social gatherings without panic taking over.

One evening, after a successful presentation at work, she called me up. I could hear her smile over the phone and she said, "I finally understand, anxiety isn't my enemy. It's just an action signal I need to pay attention to. And I can choose how I respond." She had learned a powerful truth; emotional management isn't about being emotionless. It's about reclaiming control over your reactions and refusing to let feelings dictate your life.

Through this process, she discovered freedom; the freedom to live fully, act intentionally, and pursue her life without fear holding her back.

Here's How to Become the Driver of Your Emotions

1. Your Emotional State Is Not a Mystery — It's a Pattern

People love to say, "I don't know why I feel this way."

But if you slow down and pay attention, you'll notice something. Your emotions follow a rhythm. A pattern. A script.

Somebody says something you don't like; you shut down. Plans change, you become anxious. You get challenged; you get defensive.

These aren't random reactions.

They are habits. Emotional habits you've rehearsed for years.

So, here's the key:

Whatever you practice emotionally becomes your emotional home.

If you rehearse stress, you'll live in stress. If you rehearse calmness, calm becomes your baseline. If you rehearse confidence, life eventually has no choice but to match you.

So, the real question is: What emotional address have you been living at and is it time to move?

2. Reaction Is Easy. Regulation Is True Power.

Most people do not respond to life…they react to it.

It's survival mode. It's the same emotional loop you've run since childhood. Regulation is different. Regulation is: Awareness + Intention + Ownership.

It is the moment you catch yourself about to repeat an old pattern, and instead you shift gears.

You breathe. You recentre. You choose your state instead of collapsing into your default one.

That is emotional power. That is real leadership.

Anyone can react. Leaders regulate.

This is not about being emotionless. It is about being emotionally intelligent, feeling everything, but choosing what leads you in the moment.

3. Physiology: It Is the Fastest Way in or Out of Any Emotion

Believe it or not, before you ever 'think' an emotion, your body is already shifting. Your breathing changes. Your posture collapses or expands. Your muscles tighten or release. That is why you can tell someone's emotional state before they say a word; their body broadcasts it early.

But here's the cheat code:

You can reverse-engineer your emotional state by changing your physiology first.

- ✓ ***Change your breathing, your biochemistry changes.***
- ✓ ***Change your posture, your confidence changes.***
- ✓ ***Change your movement, your momentum changes.***
- ✓ ***When your mind is chaotic, just move.***

Stand tall. Shake it out. Walk. Breathe deeper.

Break the pattern.

Your body is the remote control for your emotions. ***Use it!***

4. The Language You Use Creates the Emotions You Experience

People don't realize how much their words control their feelings.

Say *"I'm overwhelmed"* enough times, and your nervous system will believe it.

Say *"I'm stuck,"* and your brain stops looking for options.

Say *"I can't,"* and your body shuts down.

Your internal language becomes your emotional lens.

Now try this:

- ✓ ***"I'm not overwhelmed...I'm just being stretched."***
- ✓ ***"I'm not stuck...I'm pausing before my next move."***
- ✓ ***"I'm not failing...I'm learning."***

Same experience. Different story. Different emotions.

Your words are not labels. They are commands.

Speak like someone leading themselves, not losing themselves.

5. Meaning — The Switch Behind Every Emotion

Every emotion you feel boils down to one thing; what meaning did you attach to the moment?

If someone doesn't call you back, you can tell yourself, "They don't care about me" or "They're busy". One meaning creates insecurity, the other creates calm. If a challenge shows up, you can tell yourself: "This is the worst thing to happen" or "This is preparing me for the next level". One meaning weakens you. The other strengthens you. The most powerful emotional question you can ask is: ***"What else could this mean?"*** That one question breaks emotional patterns instantly. It forces your brain to access resources your fear was blocking.

You can't always control the event. But you can always control the meaning you give the event or experience.

And your meaning controls the emotion, which controls the action, which in turn controls the outcome. This is how inner mastery becomes outer mastery.

6. Emotional Management Is Not Suppression — It's Precision

People think mastering their emotions means shutting them off.

No. That is emotional avoidance, not power. Management is when you can feel anger without becoming destructive, feel fear without becoming paralyzed, feel sadness without losing yourself, feel uncertainty without retreating.

You don't run from your emotions. You listen to them. Decode them. Then direct them.

Emotion becomes information, not identity.

Stop saying, "This is just how I am," and start saying, "This is how I choose to be."

7. **The Highest Level of Emotional Management: Your State**

At the top of this mountain is a simple truth:

Your state is a choice.

Not a reaction. Not a guess. A choice.

- ✓ ***If you want clarity, choose calm.***
- ✓ ***If you want courage, choose certainty.***
- ✓ ***If you want productivity, choose focus.***
- ✓ ***If you want connection, choose presence.***
- ✓ ***If you want progress, choose hunger.***

You stop waiting to 'feel ready'. You generate readiness.

You stop waiting for motivation. You produce momentum.

You stop letting moods decide your day. You decide the mood you need and embody it.

This is the moment you step from victim. To the author. From the reactor. To the creator. From emotional survival. To emotional sovereignty. And once you reach that level, nothing outside of you can control you.

Not people. Not circumstances. Not fear. Not pressure. Your inner world becomes untouchable. And when your inner world is mastered, your outer world rearranges itself to match you.

■■■

Chapter 7
WHY WE DO WHAT WE DO

'Behaviour makes sense when you understand the need it's trying to meet.'

Every choice you've ever made, every risk, every retreat, every victory, every self-sabotage, every relationship you held onto too long, every opportunity you walked away from, was driven by one thing: *A need.*

Imagine this, people are posting and sharing around a life that, on social media, looks 'correct'. Good job. Nice car. Steady relationship. People looked at them posting and assumed they are doing well. But I can tell you, many are exhausted; mentally, emotionally, and spiritually. Many feel like running, but they don't even know towards what. For the past decade working with numerous clients from different walks of life, race, religion, class etc. I always see patterns that millions of people all around the world fall into, and that pattern and behaviour is coming from one place; ***unmet needs.***

One day a lady came to me–well spoken, wonderful family, great job, a wonderful career. Growing up, her childhood home was unpredictable. Some weeks were peaceful and some were full of chaos. Without realizing it, she spent adulthood chasing stability–steady job, strict routines, predictable days. ***Certainty*** made her feel safe. But, also too much certainty made her feel trapped.

This other person, his life was so rigid, he craved excitement in different ways. He started jumping from project to project, activities to activities, gym for three weeks, business ideas every other Tuesday. Not because he was irresponsible, but because his soul was starving for ***Variety.*** He needed a spark. He needed something to wake him up.

Another deep one some people grew up hearing was, 'you hadda make something of yourself'. Every achievement gave them a temporary high. Every compliment made them feel alive. But it never lasted. Most people realized they weren't living for meaning, they were actually living to be seen.

It wasn't working for purpose; it was working for applause. ***Significance*** became their silent addiction.

Yet others were suffering, not because they did not love their partner, but because they did not know how to let someone into their world fully. They offered support but never vulnerability. They gave presence but not emotional honesty. They cared deeply but didn't know how to express it.

They chased significance outside because they didn't know how to receive ***Love and Connection.***

Growth: This is the need that kept whispering to a lot of people during long nights. They felt guilty because they had ***'everything',*** yet were still unhappy. But the real issue was, they weren't growing anymore. Every day felt like a repeat. The same conversations. The same responsibilities. The same version of themselves. The soul was begging for evolution.

This one is the highest un-met need of all that everyone ignores without realizing it. The absence of something in your life that makes you feel like you are making an impact. No mentorship. No volunteering. No creative outlet that serves others. You are just surviving, not ***contributing.*** Achieving, but not creating meaning. And that is why life feels empty.

CHECK POINT

The moment you see your life through the ***six human needs,*** everything will click.

You weren't broken. You are not lazy. You are not confused.

You are simply unbalanced.

Sometimes we overfeed some needs and starve others. Too much certainty. Too much craving for significance. Not enough connection. Not enough growth. No contribution at all.

Once you understand this, you'll begin to redesign your life intentionally. You can add morning routines for growth. Practice honesty and vulnerability for connection. Take on youth mentorship for contribution. Align your work with purpose instead of approval.

Little by little, you will feel more alive again. Not because life changed, but because you changed how you lived it. And you will finally understand something most people spend their whole lives never realizing. You do not act based on who you are. You act based on what your human needs demand. When you meet those needs in healthy ways, your whole life rises.

It may sound simple, but it is true. Not desire. Not preference. A need. A force inside you so powerful it shapes your decisions before you are even aware a decision existed. We like to believe we are logical beings; that we calculate, weigh the pros and cons, 'think it through'. But the truth is simpler and far more confronting. We make decisions to meet our deepest human needs, and we justify them with logic after.

When you understand the needs that drive you, you understand your patterns. When you understand your patterns, you understand your life. And when you understand your life, you finally gain the power to change it.

This chapter is your mirror. Your reset button. Your breakthrough is waiting to happen. Let us dive deep into the six forces that run your life.

THE SIX HUMAN NEEDS
The Invisible Engine of Human Behaviour

These six needs are not wants; they are universal drivers. Across every culture, every background, every personality type, every success story, every downfall, the needs are the same.

What is different is how you learned to meet them. When your life feels stuck, it's not because something is wrong with you, it's because the way you are meeting your needs is no longer aligned with the person you are becoming.

Understanding these six needs gives you clarity on:

- ☐ ***Why you act the way you do.***
- ☐ ***Why others behave the way they do.***
- ☐ ***Why certain relationships thrive and others collapse.***
- ☐ ***Why you rise and why you fall.***
- ☐ ***Why you settle and why you breakout.***

This is the cheat code to human behaviour.

Let us break them down.

1. Certainty – The Need for Safety and Control

Every human being needs to feel safe. We need to know we can avoid pain and have some sense of stability and comfort.

We seek certainty through:

- ☑ ***routine***
- ☑ ***income***
- ☑ ***relationships***
- ☑ ***food***
- ☑ ***rituals***
- ☑ ***even our excuses***

Certainty is why people stay in jobs they hate or the relationships that hurt. Why do they repeat the same stories? 'This is just who I am'.

When certainty becomes your master, your future becomes your prison. But certainty is not the enemy. It becomes powerful when you create it internally instead of needing it externally.

Real certainty sounds like:

- ☑ ***'I trust myself.'***
- ☑ ***'Whatever comes, I can handle it.'***

That is the stability no one can take from you.

2. Variety – The Need for Surprise and Change

As much as we want stability, we also need unpredictability to feel alive. Variety brings excitement, novelty, and spontaneity.

We meet this need through:

- ☑ ***adventure***
- ☑ ***change***
- ☑ ***creativity***
- ☑ ***risk***
- ☑ ***new relationships***
- ☑ ***distractions***

When variety is missing, people create chaos. When variety is unmanaged, people destroy stability. Balanced variety gives life its spark. You need enough change to grow, but not so much that you lose yourself.

3. Significance — The Need to Feel Important and Valued

Every human being wants to matter. To be seen. To feel unique. To feel like their presence makes a difference.

Significance can be met in empowering ways:

- ☑ ***mastery***
- ☑ ***contribution***
- ☑ ***excellence***
- ☑ ***leadership***
- ☑ ***growth***

And it can also be met in destructive ways:

- ☐ ***drama***
- ☐ ***conflict***
- ☐ ***control***
- ☐ ***superiority***
- ☐ ***titles without substance***

When someone feels invisible, they will create a story that gets them seen, even if it destroys everything around them. Your significance becomes healthy when it's rooted in purpose, not comparison.

4. Love and Connection — The Need for Relationship and Bonding

Every human being needs to feel connected–to people, to themselves, or to something bigger.

Love and connection are met through:

- ☑ ***intimacy***
- ☑ ***compassion***
- ☑ ***friendship***
- ☑ ***shared purpose***
- ☑ ***spirituality***
- ☑ ***presence***

When this need goes unmet, loneliness becomes the quiet poison that slowly erodes identity.

But here's the shift: Love becomes powerful when you stop chasing it externally and start cultivating it internally. Self-connection is the foundation of every healthy relationship.

The first four needs are the needs of the personality. Everyone meets them, even in unhealthy ways.

The last two needs create a life of fulfilment. They are the needs of the spirit.

Few people consistently meet them, but when you do, your life becomes extraordinary.

5. Growth – The Need to Expand, Evolve, And Rise

Growth is the antidote to stagnation. If you're not growing, you're dying. If you're not evolving, you're repeating the same loop.

Growth shows up as:

☑ ***learning***

☑ ***developing new skills***

☑ ***emotional maturity***

☑ ***healing***

☑ ***self-reflection***

This need is why success feels empty if you're not growing. It is why comfort zones feel safe but suffocating. Growth is where your power lives. When you grow, everything in your life must reorganize to match your new identity.

6. Contribution – The Need to Give Beyond Yourself

This is the highest human need, the one that gives meaning to everything else.

Contribution is when your life stops being about accumulation and starts being about impact.

We meet this need by:

- ☑ ***serving***
- ☑ ***teaching***
- ☑ ***helping***
- ☑ ***guiding***
- ☑ ***mentoring***
- ☑ ***raising others***
- ☑ ***leaving fingerprints on the world***

You become unstoppable when your life is no longer driven by what you can get…*but by what you can give.*

Contribution transforms achievement into fulfilment.

So Which Need Runs Your Life?

Everyone values all six needs, but your life is shaped by the two you prioritize most.

If you value certainty and significance above all else, you'll play small and protect your ego. If you value variety and love, you may chase emotion over direction. When your top two needs become growth and contribution, you enter the rare category of people whose lives expand continuously.

Your destiny is shaped the moment you upgrade the needs that run your decisions.

CHECK POINT

The moment you understand these six needs, three things happen:

1. You understand yourself at a deeper level than ever before. *Your patterns make sense. Your triggers make sense. Your habits make sense.*

2. You understand others. *You stop taking things personally because you see the need behind the behaviour.*

3. You unlock the freedom to change.

Once you recognize your driving force, you can redirect your energy to become the person you were designed to be.

This is the foundation of emotional mastery.

This is the root of behavioural change.

This is the blueprint of fulfilment.

SECRET LEVEL

1. Which of the six needs has been controlling your decisions lately?

    Certainty? Variety? Significance? Love? Growth? Contribution?

    ____

    ____

    ____

    ____

2. Are you meeting that need in a way that lifts you or limits you?

    ____

    ____

    ____

    ____

3. What must your top two needs be now, for your life to transform?

4. What would shift in your life if you made growth and contribution your top two needs?

Take a moment.

Answer honestly.

■■■

Chapter 8

THE 7 AREAS FOR AN EXTRAORDINARY LIFE

'An extraordinary life isn't built in one area; it's sustained by alignment across all of them.'

Extraordinary lives are not built by accident. They're crafted and shaped, intentionally, one choice at a time. Every breakthrough, every shift, every leap forward comes from mastering the seven areas that quietly govern the quality of your life. When you understand these seven pillars of life and work on them consistently life stops feeling random. You stop feeling pulled in a thousand directions. You begin to rise from the inside out.

In 2019, while awaiting my flight back home to Trinidad, I met a Vice President of sales. She worked at a multinational company from Barbados and had dedicated over a decade of her life to her company. She loved her team, cherished their growth, and prided herself on being the leader who 'went the extra mile'.

But over the years, she began to feel exhausted, frustrated, and disconnected, not from her job or role, but from herself.

She realized she had been so focused on her career, that she had neglected the other critical areas of her life. She rarely exercised, skipped meals, and sacrificed sleep. Her relationships with friends and family were distant because she was always 'too busy' or 'too tired'. Even her passion for sales and marketing, which once lit up her mornings, had dimmed.

So, we chatted while awaiting our respective flights. After returning to Barbados, she decided to enrol in my coaching program. When we began working together, she discovered that she had been focusing only on one level of her life, skills and achievement. She had neglected the foundational layers, ***health, emotional awareness, personal growth, and purpose.*** Without these, her success felt hollow.

Together, we created a M.A.P.

- ☑ ***Health and Energy:*** *She committed to small, daily routines; walking in the morning, preparing simple healthy meals, and establishing a consistent sleep schedule.*

- ☑ ***Emotional Awareness:*** *She started journaling to process stress and reflect on her feelings, creating space to manage frustration before it became burnout.*

- ☑ ***Relationships:*** *She reconnected with family and friends, setting boundaries at work to allow for meaningful time outside her classroom.*

- ☑ ***Purpose and Growth:*** *She reintroduced herself to projects she loved, like creative storytelling and community mentorship, reminding herself why she became a leader in the first place.*

At first, balancing all these layers felt unnatural to her. She struggled to honour boundaries, felt guilty for taking time for herself, and worried about letting others down. But slowly, the transformation became undeniable. Her energy returned. Her creativity in the boardroom sparked again. Relationships became warmer, more connected. And for the first time in years, she felt in control of her life, not just her career, but her entire existence.

She realized a powerful truth, that her life isn't about excelling in one area while neglecting the rest. Real success comes from balance, building every layer of your life, like a pyramid. By addressing health, emotions, relationships, and purpose alongside her career, she had finally unlocked sustainable fulfilment. Her job was no longer draining, it was energizing. And she could feel pride, joy, and success that extended far beyond the boardroom.

Now, let's dive into the seven areas that separate people who merely exist from those who expand and grow.

1. Health – The Foundation of Peak Living

Everything in your life flows through your body. Your energy, your drive, your presence, your ability to show up for others; it all begins here. Your health isn't just about fitness. It's about vitality, longevity, clarity. It is the discipline of caring for the one vehicle you're guaranteed for life.

When your body is strong, your decisions are stronger. When your mind is clear, your path becomes clearer. Extraordinary lives demand extraordinary energy and energy is a choice, not luck.

2. Meaning and Emotions – Mastering the Inner World

Your life is shaped by the meaning you attach to the experience you live. Two people can go through the same situation; one collapses, one grows. What separates them is interpretation.

Master your meaning, and you master your emotions. Master your emotions, and you master your life. This is the silent battlefield where most people lose. But when you learn to direct your focus, challenge your narratives, and transform your internal language, you reclaim the power that was always yours.

Your outer world can only be as stable as your inner world.

3. Relationships – The Mirrors That Shape Us

Nothing impacts the quality of your life faster than the quality of your relationships.

Choose people who:

- ☑ ***challenge your excuses***
- ☑ ***respect your boundaries***
- ☑ ***celebrate your growth, and***
- ☑ ***refuse to let you shrink.***

Grow your connections intentionally. Protect your peace fiercely. And never apologize for wanting soul-aligned relationships.

4. Time – The Currency You Can Never Re-earn

You can make back your money. You can rebuild confidence. But time? Once it's gone, it's gone.

Most people don't lack ambition, they lack allocation.

Your life moves in the direction of what you prioritize, not what you hope for. When you learn to manage your time, you begin to manage your destiny. Because time is not something you manage, it's something you command.

Guard it.

Plan it.

Invest it wisely.

5. Career – Purpose in Motion

Your career is not just about earning an income, it's about expressing your gifts.

It's about impact, alignment, and contribution.

You're here to grow, not to settle.

To expand, not exist.

To build a life that feels meaningful, not mechanical.

When your work reflects your values, your confidence rises. When your skills grow, your opportunities multiply. And when you operate from purpose, your path becomes unstoppable.

6. Money – A Tool That Magnifies Who You Are

Money is not the root of evil or the source of happiness. *It is a mirror. It reflects your habits, your discipline, your beliefs, your identity.*

You don't chase money; you attract it through the person you become.

Mastering money is mastering:

- ☑ ***discipline,***
- ☑ ***emotional control,***
- ☑ ***delayed gratification,***
- ☑ ***intelligent decisions,***
- ☑ ***and resourcefulness.***

Wealth amplifies your impact. It gives you options. It gives you freedom. It allows you to build, not just survive.

7. Giving Back – The Path to Fulfilment

Growth without contribution feels empty. Success without service collapses inward.

There is a unique joy that only comes from giving, *a fulfilment* no achievement can match.

When you serve others, you expand your soul. When you uplift others, you uplift yourself. When you contribute, life returns the favour in ways you could never predict.

The happiest people are not the ones who have the most, they're the ones who give the most.

Because life always responds to generosity.

Now let's bring all the areas of your life together.

The extraordinary life isn't built in one moment, it's built through daily discipline in these seven areas.

- ☑ ***Your health fuels you.***
- ☑ ***Your meaning and emotions guide you.***
- ☑ ***Your relationships support you.***
- ☑ ***Your time shapes you.***
- ☑ ***Your career expresses you.***
- ☑ ***Your money empowers you.***
- ☑ ***Your service fulfils you.***

When all seven rise, your entire life rises. This is the blueprint of a life that doesn't just succeed; it expands, it inspires, and it transforms everyone it touches.

CHECK POINT:

The Seven-Area Self-Assessment

Use this exercise to slow down, scan your life honestly, and identify where your next breakthrough is waiting.

Take your time with each section.

Your clarity begins here.

1. **Health –** ***What is my energy telling me?***

Reflect:

- ☐ ***How do I truly feel in my body right now?***
- ☐ ***What habits drain me?***
- ☐ ***What habits fuel me?***
- ☐ ***What is one shift I can make this week to strengthen my energy?***

Write it down clearly.

3. **Meaning and Emotions – What story am I living in?**

Reflect:

- ☐ ***What meaning do I give to the challenges in my life?***
- ☐ ***What emotion do I find myself experiencing most often?***
- ☐ ***What emotion do I want to create more intentionally?***

Choose one new meaning you are ready to install.

____

____

____

____

3. **Relationships – Who helps me rise?**

Reflect:

- ☐ ***Which relationships energize me?***
- ☐ ***Which ones exhaust me?***
- ☐ ***Where have I allowed poor boundaries?***
- ☐ ***What is one relationship upgrade I'm ready to make?***

Define your next relational standard.

4. **Time – Where is my time leaking?**

Reflect:

- ☐ ***What steals my time without adding value?***
- ☐ ***What matters that I've been postponing?***
- ☐ ***What is one commitment I must put back into my schedule?***

Identify the shift that will change everything.

6. **Career – Am I growing or settling?**

Reflect:

- ☐ ***Does my current work reflect my deepest values?***
- ☐ ***Am I expanding my skills or repeating my years?***
- ☐ ***What would 'next level' look like for me?***

Write one action that moves you toward purpose.

____

____

____

____

6. **Money – What belief controls my financial life?**

Reflect:

- ☐ ***What is my earliest memory of money?***
- ☐ ***How has that shaped my current decisions?***
- ☐ ***Am I avoiding, overspending, or playing small?***

Choose one empowering financial behaviour to begin this week.

7. **Giving Back – Where can I serve more?**

Reflect:

- ☐ ***Who could benefit from my experience, kindness, or presence?***
- ☐ ***What simple act of service can I commit to?***
- ☐ ***How can I build a contribution into my daily or weekly life?***

Decide one act of service you'll practice intentionally.

RESET POINT:

Your Life Audit Score

From 1–10, rate each area honestly with *1 as the lowest and 10 as the highest rank*:

- ☐ Health ____________
- ☐ Meaning and Emotions ____________
- ☐ Relationships ____________
- ☐ Time ____________
- ☐ Career ____________
- ☐ Money ____________
- ☐ Giving Back ____________

Circle the lowest number. This is your breakthrough.

Final Activation Question

"If I improved just ONE of these areas over the next 30 days, which one would create the biggest ripple in my life, and what is the first step I will take?"

Write it. Commit to it. Begin.

____

____

____

■■■

Chapter 9

BE CAREFUL OF YOUR SOURCE

'When your worth is sourced externally, your peace will always be negotiable.'

There has never been a time in human history where information was this accessible. Every day you are surrounded by voices; online, offline, in conversations, in comments, in culture. And the danger is this, when everything is loud, anything can start to sound like the truth. And it is showing up a lot and creating more uneasiness among a lot of people, old and young.

I recall recently a young lady who reached out to me on a social media platform to see if I could help her overcome her anxiety and stress. When we spoke and I offered my cost she replied plainly: "Mr. Best I can't afford you right now."

This young woman started a new job with excitement and ambition. She loved the idea of contributing, learning, and growing in her career. But within a few months, the environment began to take a toll on her.

The office was filled with negativity. Gossip flowed freely. Complaints were constant. Every small mistake, whether hers or someone else's, became a topic for criticism and ridicule. Meetings often felt like arenas of judgment rather than collaboration.

At first, she tried to adapt. She told herself: "This is just how workplaces are. I need to toughen up." But day by day, the stress and anxiety mounted. She found herself dreading emails, avoiding colleagues, and leaving the office feeling drained and hollow.

It did not take long before she realized the problem wasn't her skill or effort, it was the sources she was allowing into her mind. Constant exposure to negativity, criticism, and toxic energy was eroding her confidence, focus, and emotional well-being.

After analysing and understanding her situation, I made a decision and a commitment to work with her for ***free.*** I just could not allow such a bright and beautiful soul to fall because of the system she lived and worked in. The only investment I asked of her was her time, and she showed up to every single session for four weeks, and through my coaching, she learned a vital lesson; protecting your mental health isn't passive, it requires intentional choices about what and who we let influence us daily.

I taught her how to start setting boundaries, so she limited participation in gossip-filled conversations, choosing to remain neutral or walk away. I showed her how to seek out new voices, supportive colleagues, and mentors who offered constructive feedback instead of tearing her down. I taught her mental rituals at the start and end of each day, grounding herself and reinforcing a positive mindset before engaging with the workplace.

The change wasn't immediate. She still had to navigate a challenging environment, but her relationship with it shifted. Instead of absorbing negativity, she observed it, learned from constructive input, and let go of what didn't serve her.

Within the four weeks I worked with her, her stress levels dropped, her productivity increased, and she regained a sense of peace. Most importantly, she discovered that mental health is a currency, and guarding your sources is like safeguarding your wealth. By choosing what she exposed herself to; whether people, media, or conversations, she regained control over her energy, focus, and happiness. The workplace remained the same, but she had transformed her experience within it.

Every day, someone or something is speaking into you.

A voice.

A message.

A belief.

A tone.

A fear.

A hope.

Most people don't realize it, but your life is being shaped by the sources you drink from. Your inner world is a reflection of the voices you trust, the opinions you absorb, and the environments you allow to influence your truth.

This chapter is your wake-up call.

It's not to judge anyone. Or to isolate yourself.

It is for you to be intentional about the wells you draw water from on a daily basis because not every well carries clean water. Not every source can sustain your spirit. Not every voice deserves a seat inside your mind.

The Invisible Feeds That Shape Your Reality

There are three major sources that shape people daily:

1. ***People***
2. ***Environments***
3. ***Internal Scripts***

And each of these can either lift you higher or drain your energy, clarity, and confidence.

1. People:

Human beings pick up emotional contagion just like we pick up the common cold. Spend enough *time* around fear-filled people; you'll inherit their panic. Spend enough *time* around dreamers; you'll start thinking about possibilities. Spend enough *time* around bitter people; you'll begin to question your own joy.

RESET POINT:

- ☑ ***Who do I allow to influence my decisions?***
- ☑ ***Do they feed my courage or feed my insecurities?***
- ☑ ***Do they speak life or drain life?***
- ☑ ***Do they believe in growth or do they cling to limitations?***

You don't need perfect people around you. But you do need people who speak truth, not manipulation. People who offer clarity, not confusion. People who see your potential, not your failures. People who correct with love, not crush with judgment.

Be careful of the *people-source.*

A weak voice in your environment becomes a loud voice in your head.

2. Environments:

Your environment is a living ecosystem. Even in silence, it is feeding you information. The energy in your home. The morale in your workplace. The tone of your social media feed. The culture of the rooms you walk into. The expectations of the people you spend time with.

If the rooms you choose normalize *complaining, chaos, gossip, excuses, or negativity,* don't be surprised when you start feeling heavy, confused, or disconnected from yourself. And if the rooms you are in celebrate *growth, accountability, gratitude, and belief,* don't be surprised when your life elevates.

Your environment writes half your story before you ever make a decision. This is why one shift in the environment can change your entire destiny.

Be careful of the *environment-source.*

It whispers louder than you think.

3. Internal Scripts:

There's a voice inside you that plays 24/7. It's not always loud. But it is constant. Your internal script becomes your compass.

And that script is built from:

- ☑ ***Childhood experiences***
- ☑ ***Repeated messages***
- ☑ ***Past trauma***
- ☑ ***Unhealed moments***
- ☑ ***Moments of success***
- ☑ ***Conditioning and patterns***

When that inner voice is fractured, even the good around you, feels threatening.

When it's empowered, even the chaos around you feels manageable.

RESET POINT:

- ☐ ***What story am I telling myself daily?***
- ☐ ***Does it free me or imprison me?***
- ☐ ***Does it expand me or shrink me?***
- ☐ ***Is this voice my truth or someone else's programming?***

Be careful of the *internal-source.*

It becomes the architect of your future.

THE SPIRITUAL SOURCE:

There is one source that cannot be corrupted, manipulated, or exhausted. A source that remains steady when people fail. A source that remains pure when environments fluctuate. A source that remains truthful when your inner voice becomes noisy.

It is the spiritual source, your divine connection.

Call it: *God, The Universe, The Creator, The Divine, Your Higher Self, Spirit, The Source of Life.* Whatever your language, the principle remains the same. There is a higher intelligence that can feed you clarity, peace, direction, and strength in ways no human voice ever can.

This source speaks in:

- ☑ ***Stillness***
- ☑ ***Intuition***
- ☑ ***Conviction***
- ☑ ***Alignments***
- ☑ ***Lessons***
- ☑ ***Synchronicities***
- ☑ ***Quiet knowing***

When you tap into this source, you're not just listening. You are being filled.

☑ ***You start walking with discernment.***

☑ ***You sense what's real and what's noise.***

☑ ***You identify manipulation faster.***

☑ ***You detach from opinions easier.***

☑ ***You feel guided instead of guessing.***

☑ ***You operate from purpose instead of pressure.***

The spiritual source is not loud. It is not dramatic. It's not built on ego. It is built on truth, and truth does not need volume to stand strong.

When the *spiritual source* becomes your foundation, every other source must pass through your discernment filter. This is the power you've been needing.

Who or What is Feeding You?

To protect your mind, heart, and spirit, ask yourself these questions regularly:

1. ***Does this voice lift me or lower me?*** *If it drains your peace, it's not your source.*

2. ***Does this person speak truth or manipulate?*** *Honesty builds you. Manipulation breaks you.*

3. ***Does this environment help me grow or keep me stuck?*** *You cannot elevate in a place designed for survival.*

4. ***Is my inner voice speaking from wounds or wisdom?*** *Healing upgrades your inner source.*

5. ***Do I feel closer to clarity or confusion after listening?*** *Confusion is a sign of misalignment.*

6. ***Does this align with my spiritual truth?*** *If it violates your soul, it's not for you.*

My Message to You

Your life will always rise to the quality of the sources you trust. Guard your mind like a fortress. Protect your spirit like sacred ground. Honor your peace like a priceless asset. And above all, stay connected to the one source that never leads you wrong.

When you choose your *source wisely,* you choose your future wisely.

CHECK POINT:

Take a moment to evaluate your current influences.

Part 1: People Audit

List the five people you interact with the most.

Next to each name write one of these three points:

- ☐ ***Feeds Me***
- ☐ ***Drains Me***
- ☐ ***Neutral***

Ask yourself 'why'.

Part 2: Environment Audit

List the three environments you spend the most time in. Write one word from the following list that describes how each environment makes you feel.

- ☐ ***Energized***
- ☐ ***Heavy***
- ☐ ***Inspired***
- ☐ ***Distracted***

Part 3: Inner Voice Audit

Write down three repeating thoughts you've had this week. Are they empowering or limiting? Where do they come from?

____

____

____

____

____

____

____

____

Part 4: Spiritual Alignment

Write down one moment this week where you felt guided, peaceful, or deeply aware.

What was that moment trying to tell you?

Part 5: Integration

Write a short statement:

"Going forward, these are the sources I will trust and these are the sources I will release."

Let this chapter be the filter that protects your future.

Your life deserves clean, strong, nourishing sources. Choose them with intention.

■■■

Chapter 10
THIS IS THE FASTEST WAY:
To Lose Your Peace

'Peace isn't found by controlling life, but by choosing what you no longer fight.'

Most people walk through life with a quiet list of rules in their head, rules about how others should speak, support, behave, love, notice, understand, or respond. We rarely say these rules out loud, but we expect life to follow them. And when life doesn't, frustration rises, disappointment grows and stress multiplies.

I remember working with a client from New York, a program director at a major media network. She dedicated herself to her job for over two decades. She spent countless years building and working on her career to be successful in it. Yet, despite all her success, recognition was rare. A simple 'thank you' from a colleague was almost non-existent. She felt invisible, undervalued, and exhausted.

Every day, she carried a weight of ***expectation*** that her hard work should automatically be acknowledged. And when it was not, frustration built. She began questioning her worth, her contributions, and even her choice to remain in the company. During our sessions, we explored the impact of these expectations. She realized her unhappiness wasn't caused by the lack of appreciation itself, it was caused by the belief that appreciation had to come from others to validate her efforts.

We worked on shifting her ***focus***, reframing her mindset. She began seeing her efforts as intrinsically valuable, not dependent on external acknowledgment. Celebrating her impact, she started keeping a journal of small victories; systems she created, improved quality and production, colleagues who smiled, moments of genuine connection.

By shifting her energy, instead of waiting for 'thanks', she put energy into being fully present and giving her best work for its own sake. At first, the change felt strange. The habits of expectation were deeply ingrained, and old frustrations surfaced frequently. But slowly, she began experiencing a different kind of fulfilment; a quiet, steady joy that came from knowing she was making a real difference, regardless of whether anyone noticed.

By ***appreciating*** more, and ***expecting*** less she

discovered freedom. Working no longer felt like a burden or a battle for recognition; it became a source of satisfaction, pride, and purpose.

She learned a powerful lesson. True fulfilment comes from valuing the impact of your actions, not waiting for others to validate them. In embracing this shift, she regained her energy, her passion, and her confidence and found that life feels lighter when you give without expecting anything in return. **No Expectations**!

So, what is the fastest way to lose your peace? It's ***Expectations***.

It doesn't come with fanfare, and you often don't notice it until it has already stolen your peace. It lives in your mind as a quiet demand: *'This should happen', 'They should act this way', or 'I deserve this outcome'*. The problem is not the desire itself; it is the mental rigidity that attaches your peace to an outcome beyond your control.

When you expect, you unconsciously place your happiness, calm, and sense of self-worth in the hands of people, circumstances, or the future. And when reality doesn't match your expectation, frustration, disappointment, resentment, and even anger arise.

Here's the truth: Expectation is a form of resistance to what is. It is a refusal to fully engage with the present. The more rigid your expectations, the more often you will experience life as unfair, difficult, or disappointing.

Why We Expect

Expectations often stem from beliefs, past experiences, or social conditioning.

Beliefs about how life 'should' be: ***'Success looks like this, love should feel like this, people should act like that.'***

Fear of disappointment

We expect to prevent being hurt or let down, ironically creating the very disappointment we fear.

Control illusions

We expect in the hope that we can shape outcomes, not realizing control is always limited. The irony is that by expecting, you often push life further away instead of allowing it to flow naturally. Peace and expectation rarely coexist.

Here's how to release expectations.

The key to reclaiming your peace is not lowering your *standards or ambitions*, it is learning to separate your sense of well-being from the outcome of external events. Life is always unfolding, and your peace is your choice, not the result of circumstances.

Here are practical steps to begin releasing expectation:

1. ***Awareness:*** *Notice where you are expecting someone or something to behave or occur a certain way. Awareness is the first step toward freedom.*
2. ***Acceptance:*** *Remind yourself that reality is not obligated to meet your mental image of how things should be. Say to yourself: "This is what is, not what I thought it should be."*
3. ***Focus on what you control:*** *Your actions, responses, and mindset are within your control. The rest is not.*
4. ***Shift your lens:*** *Move from expecting to allowing. Instead of demanding life to follow a script, stay present with it and respond authentically.*

SECRET LEVEL:

Releasing Expectations

Step 1: Identify Your Expectations

Take a moment to write down THREE areas of your life where you feel frustrated or tense. For each, ask yourself:

- ☐ ***What am I expecting here?***
- ☐ ***Who or what is not meeting my expectations?***

Step 2: Track the Cost

For each expectation, write down how it affects your peace, your mood, and your energy. Notice the subtle ways your expectation is stealing joy.

Step 3: Reframe

Next to each expectation, write a neutral or accepting statement. For example:

Instead of: "They should appreciate me," **write** "I can appreciate myself regardless of how others act."

Instead of: "This deal should go my way," **write** "I will do my best and accept the outcome."

Step 4: Practice Daily

Every morning, set an intention: "Today, I will release the need for things to be a certain way. I choose peace over expectation."

Notice throughout the day when expectation arises, and gently return to acceptance.

Step 5: Reflect Weekly

At the end of the week, journal about any moments where you successfully released expectations. How did your energy and peace shift?

CHECK POINT:

Expectation is the fastest route to frustration and disappointment. Peace, however, is available the moment you choose to release the ***'shoulds'*** and live fully in the reality of what is. True freedom comes when you no longer gamble your happiness on someone else's actions or the unfolding of life according to your mental script.

But appreciation?

Appreciation is one of the fastest ways to reclaim it. Appreciation changes the emotional temperature inside you. It shifts your focus from what's missing to what's meaningful, from what's wrong to what's working, from what people didn't do to what they already give.

Gratitude isn't weakness. It's a state of power.

When you appreciate, you become more resourceful, more patient, more creative, more compassionate. You stop living life with clenched fists and start living it with open hands. And here is the principle that has changed millions of lives, including my own: **Trade your expectations for appreciation.**

That shift alone can transform your entire emotional world.

It does not mean lowering your standards. It means releasing the silent demands that drain your joy. When you replace expectation with appreciation, you create space not only for gratitude, but for ***grace.*** The same situation feels lighter. The same person feels easier to love. The same problem feels smaller. Your body relaxes. Your mind opens. Your spirit strengthens.

Gratitude does not change everything around you, but it changes you, and that changes how you move through everything.

Today, challenge yourself to look again. Look at the people, the moments, the opportunities you normally rush past.

- ☐ ***What have you been overlooking?***
- ☐ ***What beauty have you been too busy to see?***
- ☐ ***What blessing have you allowed to become ordinary?***

When you train your mind to appreciate the present, you activate a different version of yourself, one that is calmer, wiser, and more tuned in to the life you're actually living.

And that version of you? That's the one capable of growth, peace, success, and connection.

SECRET LEVEL:

The Appreciation Shift

Take five to ten minutes and walk through these prompts:

1. **Where in your life have expectations been creating frustration?** Be honest. Write down one area where your silent rules have been blocking your peace.

2. **What can you appreciate about that same situation or person right now?** List at least three things big or small.

3. **Write one sentence that re-centres you in appreciation instead of expectation.** (Example: "I choose to appreciate progress, not demand perfection.")

4. **Message one person today and tell them specifically what you appreciate about them.** Notice how your energy shifts immediately after.

■■■

Chapter 11

THE ULTIMATE CHANGE CODE

'Lasting change happens when who you are finally matches what you know.'

There comes a point in every person's life when 'trying' isn't enough anymore. When repeating the same patterns, mentally, emotionally, spiritually, starts to feel like a quiet betrayal of who you know you could be. Transformation only begins the moment you stop negotiating with old habits and start designing a new identity.

A couple years ago I met a young man from San Fernando, who had grown up believing that his potential was limited by his background. His family had struggled financially, and the community often reinforced the idea that people like him 'had to accept what life gives them'.

By the time he reached adulthood, he carried those

stories deeply ingrained in his mind. Every time he tried to aim higher, applying for a better position, pitching a new idea, or pursuing further education, self-doubt and fear would creep in. Old voices whispered: "You're not ready, boy. You're not enough. You'll fail like everyone else."

He was trapped in a cycle of wanting change but being held back by the story he believed about himself. No matter how much he planned or worked, nothing seemed to stick.

When I began working with him, I introduced him to the principles of the ***Ultimate Change Code.***

I helped to identify the story that was holding him back. He wrote down every limiting belief, about his career, his worth, and what he 'couldn't do'. Seeing them on paper made the impact undeniable. He understood why it was holding him back. He traced these beliefs to their origins; childhood lessons, societal expectations, and repeated experiences of doubt and criticism. He then replaced it with empowering actions. Instead of letting fear dictate his choices, he committed to specific actions that aligned with the story he wanted to live.

He began small, enrolling in professional development courses. Speaking up in meetings at work, even when his voice trembled. Every small win challenged the old narrative. Every success, no matter how minor, chipped away at the story he had been living. Slowly, fear and self-doubt lost their grip.

Within months, he applied for and earned a leadership position he had previously thought unattainable. Recently he spoke at a community event, sharing his journey and inspiring others. He finally saw himself not as someone limited by circumstance, but as someone capable of rewriting his own story.

The lesson was clear, transformation begins when we stop letting old narratives dictate our actions. By intentionally choosing new beliefs and supporting them with consistent action, he activated the ***Ultimate Change Code*** and in doing so, he unlocked a version of himself that had always been possible but was waiting to be claimed.

That's what The Ultimate Change Code is all about, understanding the internal mechanics of real, lasting change. You see, most people think change starts with action. It does not.

Real change begins with ***state, story, and strategy,*** *in that order.*

Let's dive in a bit deeper.

1. Your State: The Invisible Engine

Your state is the foundation. When your *physiology* is low, your energy is scattered, or your emotions are tense, nothing you attempt will stick. This is why two people can receive the same opportunity and only one rises. Your state creates capacity.

When you shift your ***breathing, your posture, and your focus, you shift your power.***

In that moment, you're no longer reacting; you're rewiring.

2. Your Story: The Meaning You Live In

Every human being is living inside a story, about who they are, what they're capable of, and what their life is supposed to be. But here's the truth, stories aren't facts. They're interpretations that became familiar. And whatever story you tell yourself consistently becomes your emotional home. If you want to change your life, you must upgrade the story you live in.

Move from: 'This is just the way I am' to 'This is who I am becoming.'

Move from: 'Life keeps happening to me' to 'Life is helping me to build strength.'

The moment your story becomes empowering, your behaviours begin to align automatically.

3. Your Strategy: The Map to Move Forward

Strategy is where structure meets intention. It's not just what you do, it's how and why.

A good strategy simplifies what you want to become. A great strategy makes the path obvious. You don't need fifty habits. You need the right three.

When your state is strong, your story is aligned, and your strategy is simple and practical, change becomes inevitable, not forced.

The Real Power Behind Change

Most people do not succeed, not because they are weak. It is because they create impotent goals and they lack consistency. And they are inconsistent because they never changed their identity. Identity is the thermostat of your life. You rise or fall to whatever level your identity is set at.

The Ultimate Change Code is the process of elevating that thermostat. Not by pretending, but by training your inner world so consistently that the outside world has no choice but to adjust. Change is not a miracle. Change is a formula. And when you understand the formula, you can rewrite any area of your life.

Here's the formula:

Create leverage: *To break old patterns, you must associate massive pain with what you've done in the past and create a compelling vision of the future that links even more pain to staying the same.*

Raise your standards: *Decide to stop accepting less than you deserve and transform your 'shoulds' into 'musts' to create an unstoppable force for change.*

Interrupt limiting patterns: *Break the cycle of destructive behaviours by changing your physical and mental state instantly. This can be done by changing your body's position, breathing, or focus.*

Replace with an empowering pattern: *Once you've created the leverage and interrupted the old pattern, you need to replace it with a new, empowering one that moves you toward your goals.*

Get clear on your 'why': *Have a clear and compelling reason for the change. Your 'why' is the driving force behind your motivation and commitment.*

Take massive action: *Success requires consistent action. Focusing on your goals and taking massive action is crucial for achieving them.*

Find fulfilment: *Lasting change comes not just from achievement but also from living a fulfilling life. Balance growth with giving back to experience true happiness.*

SECRET LEVEL:

Reset Your Thermostat

Take ten minutes and write down the following:

1. **STATE –** What emotional or physical state do you fall into most often? And what state would serve you better?

2. **STORY –** What story have you been telling yourself that keeps you stuck?

3. **REWRITE** it into a story that gives you strength and possibility.

____

____

____

____

____

4. **STRATEGY –** Identify three simple, daily actions that match the identity you're stepping into.

____

____

____

____

____

____

____

____

____

____

____

5. **IDENTITY SHIFT –** Complete this sentence: "From today forward, I am the kind of person who…" This becomes the anchor for the new you.

■■■

Chapter 12

FEAR: *The Illusion That Steals Your Future*

'Fear grows in silence; courage grows in movement'

There comes a moment in every person's life when fear stops being a feeling and becomes a lifestyle, a silent agreement you never meant to sign. Not because you're weak. Not because you're incapable. But because fear disguises itself so well that you begin trusting the very thing that's limiting you.

One time while I was writing for the ***Trinidad Guardian Health Plus Magazine*** a parent reached out to me about her son. A college student from Tobago, he had always dreamed of studying abroad. From the time he was a child, he pictured himself walking across campuses in distant countries, learning, growing, and building a life full of possibilities.

But as he grew older, fear began to creep in. Fear of rejection. Fear of failure. Fear of disappointing his family and community. He imagined being denied admission, struggling to adapt, or feeling out of place in a foreign environment. Each 'what if' scenario played repeatedly in his mind, paralyzing him from taking any concrete steps toward his dream.

Years passed, and the dream remained just that, a dream. Every application form he looked at became an exercise in anxiety rather than hope. The more he feared, the less he acted, and the more his confidence eroded. When I began working with him, we identified the root of his fear; the fear of rejection had become a barrier that controlled his life. We reframed fear as a signal, not a stop sign. Fear, we agreed, was an indicator of growth, a signal that he was stepping outside his comfort zone.

We began taking deliberate, small steps; research and preparation. He carefully researched programs, admission requirements, and scholarship opportunities, building clarity and reducing uncertainty.

Action Despite Fear

He started completing applications, even though the anxiety was intense, acknowledging fear without letting it stop him. We also created a network that encouraged him while holding him accountable. Every small action chipped away at the power of fear. With each completed form, each essay drafted, he felt his courage growing. He realized that fear was only as strong as the attention he gave it, and that action, no matter how small, diluted its control.

Finally, after months of preparation and effort, he submitted his applications. The waiting period was nerve-wracking, but this time he faced it differently. He had done everything he could; the rest was out of his hands.

Then one day he received his acceptance letter; it wasn't just an invitation to study abroad, it was a powerful lesson in overcoming fear. He had learned that fear is not an enemy but a guide, signalling where growth lies. By acting in spite of it, he reclaimed control of his life and stepped into a future he had only dreamed of.

From that experience, he carried a deep understanding that fear will always appear at the edge of growth. The only way to move forward is to feel it, respect it, and ***act anyway.*** That's the essence of courage, and the key to breaking through life's biggest barriers.

Fear, at its root, is a prediction, a future fantasy, a story built on the assumption that things will go wrong. But what if fear is simply your imagination working against you? What if your mind has been rehearsing the wrong future?

The Silence That Feeds Fear

Fear thrives in stillness, not the peaceful stillness of meditation or reflection, but the paralyzing stillness of hesitation. Fear grows when you overthink, when you sit too long, when you replay the same scenario in your head without ever taking a step.

Because the longer you stay still, the more fear multiplies.

This is why fear loves silence.

When you don't speak about it.

When you don't act against it.

When you don't challenge it.

Fear Hates Movement

If fear has one weakness, one vulnerability, one crack in its armour, it is movement.

Even the smallest step disrupts fear's power; *action creates clarity, motion creates momentum, movement creates courage.*

Courage doesn't come before the step; courage awakens because of the step.

You've experienced this before:

- ☑ ***The second you finally move fear's voice gets weaker.***
- ☑ ***The second you take action your mind gets clearer.***
- ☑ ***The second you start anxiety turns into energy.***

Why? Because fear needs stillness and stagnation to survive. The moment you move, you switch from survival mode and fear gradually disappears and that is where fear dies for that period.

The Dangers of Fear

Fear does more than pause your progress. Fear reshapes your identity.

1. Fear Makes You Settle

Fear convinces you that 'good enough' is safer than 'great'. But settling is not safe, settling is slow damage. You don't feel the pain immediately, but you feel it eventually; the frustration, the resentment, the regret of knowing you were made for more but lived for less.

2. Fear Limits Your Vision

You stop dreaming boldly. You stop imagining freely. You stop seeing yourself accurately. Fear makes you forget who you are and what you carry.

3. Fear Shrinks Your World

Every time you avoid something because of fear, your world gets smaller. A smaller world means fewer opportunities. Fewer experiences. Fewer breakthroughs. Fewer chances to meet the version of you that exists on the other side of courage.

4. Fear Blocks Growth

Nothing grows in comfort. Nothing expands in hesitation. Fear keeps you exactly where you've always been, even when life is calling you higher.

5. Fear Steals Time

Fear doesn't just steal dreams. Fear steals time, the one resource you never get back. Fear makes you procrastinate on your purpose until the years pass and you look back wondering, "How much further would I be if I simply moved when I was afraid?"

Why Fear Feels Real?

Fear feels real because your brain is designed to keep you safe. The mind's job is survival, not achievement. Not growth. Not expansion.

So, your brain will always choose the familiar over the future. That's why doing something new feels scary, not because you're in danger, but because you're in unfamiliar territory.

Your brain would rather return you to an old problem than guide you into a new possibility. This is why fear feels convincing. But convincing is not the same as correct.

Fear feels real, but fear is rarely right.

How To Manage Fear and Take Your Power Back

Fear cannot be erased but it can be managed, redirected, and stripped of its authority.

Here's how you take back control:

1. **Name the Fear**

   Fear thrives in ambiguity. When you name it, you shrink it.

   Ask yourself: "What exactly am I afraid of?"

   Be specific.

   Be honest.

   Be direct.

Naming the fear brings it out of the shadows.

____

____

____

____

____

____

____

____

2. Challenge the Story

Behind every fear is a story, usually exaggerated, distorted, or inherited.

Ask yourself:

- ☐ ***"What story is this fear telling me?"***
- ☐ ***"Is this story true?"***
- ☐ ***"Who would I be without this story?"***

Most fears aren't true…

It's storytelling.

3. Move First

You don't need confidence to move.

You need movement to build confidence.

Commit to the smallest step, even two minutes of action breaks fear's pattern.

Fear hates movement.

4. Use Your Physiology

You can't stay fearful when you shift your body.

Stand tall.

Breathe deeper.

Move your energy.

Change your posture.

Your body influences your emotions more than your thoughts do.

If you want to control fear, control your physiology (Move Your Body).

5. Control Your Focus

Whatever you focus on grows. When you focus on danger, fear grows. When you focus on possibility, courage grows.

Ask yourself: "What's the best that could happen?"

Direct your mind instead of letting fear direct your life.

6. Surround Yourself with Movement

Whether it's environment, mentors, community, or pressure, movement creates movement. Stay around people who stretch you. Enter spaces that challenge you. Say 'yes' to opportunities that push you.

Fear hates growth environments.

7. Reframe Fear as Energy

Fear and excitement feel the same in the body. The only difference is the story you attach to the feeling. Instead of saying, "I'm scared," try saying, "I'm activated."

This shifts you from avoidance to readiness.

8. Remember Your History

You've survived every difficult moment in your life. You've overcome challenges you once thought would break you. Fear tries to make you forget your strength, but your history is proof that you are built for more.

- ☐ ***Your purpose requires discomfort.***
- ☐ ***Your expansion requires uncertainty.***
- ☐ ***Your next level requires motion.***

Fear will always say, "Stay and Settle."

Courage will always whisper "Move and Go."

The life you want is on the other side of movement. Not massive leaps, consistent motion. Break the silence. Interrupt the stillness. Move your body before fear moves your life. Because fear is powerless once you begin.

RESET POINT:

Reclaim Your Future from Fear

1. **Name Your Fear:** Write down one fear that has been stealing your momentum.

____

____

2. **Identify the Story:** What story has this fear been telling you? Why have you believed it?

3. **Challenge It:** Write the truth beneath the lie.

What's the reality? What's the possibility fear has been blocking you from seeing?

4. Choose One Micro-Movement

A small, simple step–something you can complete within five minutes, that goes against the fear's narrative.

5. Rewire the Identity

Finish this sentence and keep it somewhere visible:

'Courage grows in me every time I move. I am becoming the version of myself that fear can no longer control.'

■■■

Chapter 13
THE CHEAT CODE EVERYONE MUST LIVE BY

'Responsibility is the price of freedom and the gateway to becoming who you were meant to be.'

There's a point in every journey when strategy, habits, mindset, and identity all meet their limit. You can be disciplined. You can be intentional. You can do the inner work. But real power, real peace, comes from something deeper. There is a spiritual code that sits underneath everything. You become unstoppable the moment you remember you are guided.

A young woman from Maraval had always been ambitious. From an early age, she set high goals for herself, excelling in school, advancing quickly in her career, and building a life that reflected success. But no matter how hard she worked life rarely unfolded the way she expected.

Promotions were delayed, opportunities seemed to pass by, and every setback felt personal.

She carried a constant weight of frustration and worry, believing that if she did not control every outcome, she would fail. Anxiety became a daily companion, whispering that she was falling behind, missing her chance, or not 'good enough'.

When she hired me as her coach, I introduced her to a simple yet profound cheat code–spiritual grounding. She learned that life is not only about pushing, planning, and controlling, but also about alignment, trust, and connecting to something greater than oneself.

We began with small daily practices. She set aside 10–15 minutes each morning to sit quietly, breathe deeply, and centre herself before the day began. Journaling for guidance, she recorded her thoughts, fears, and intentions, listening to the inner voice that often goes unheard amid the noise of worry. Trusting the process, instead of forcing outcomes, she intentionally released attachment to results, affirming that life was unfolding according to a higher plan.

At first, the shift was subtle. She still felt impatience and doubt, but over time, she began noticing signs of clarity and synchronicity. Decisions became easier; she knew which opportunities to pursue and which to let go. Setbacks no longer crushed her; they became lessons and redirections. One afternoon she got a call from her HR manager telling her she received a promotion she had been hoping for, but not in the timeline she expected. Instead of panic or frustration, she felt calm and grateful. She understood that the delay had prepared her for a role she was now fully ready to step into, with confidence and purpose.

Through this process, she realized the power of spiritual grounding. Life does not always move on our timetable, but when we align our actions with inner guidance, the right doors open at the right time. Trusting divine timing does not mean inaction; it means acting intentionally while surrendering control over outcomes. True peace and clarity come from connection with a higher source, not from trying to force life into a script.

By adopting this cheat code, she transformed her relationship with life. Ambition and effort remained, but they were now anchored in trust and faith. Her days became lighter, her decisions more inspired, and her path more aligned with her purpose.

She finally understood that life doesn't have to be a struggle against time or circumstance. The real power comes from grounding yourself spiritually and trusting the journey.

We live in a world that worships human opinion. A world where validation has become a currency, and people chase voices that were never meant to define them. But when your spirit is anchored, you do not need the world to confirm what God already whispered inside you.

This final chapter is about that ***anchor.***

It is not about religion.

It is about aligning your connection to something wiser, higher, and steadier than your fear.

1. The Code of Stillness

Life gets loud. Your emotions get loud. People get loud. But stillness is where truth reveals itself.

When you slow your breathing, when you sit with yourself. When you stop bargaining with your doubts, you hear the part of you that is untouched by confusion.

Stillness gives clarity. And clarity gives direction.

2. The Code of Trust

Trust is not pretending everything is fine. Trust is recognizing that even when things don't make sense yet, they are still moving in your favour. Most people trust when things are good. But your spiritual strength shows up when nothing is certain and you still refuse to collapse internally.

Trust doesn't remove battles. It gives you the courage to walk through them without losing yourself.

3. The Code of Alignment

Alignment means your life stops being noisy and starts being honest. You stop forcing relationships that drain you. You stop accepting roles that shrink you. You stop compromising your peace to make others comfortable.

When you live in alignment, your spirit becomes your compass. You know when something is right, not because it's easy, but because it's true.

4. The Code of Surrender

Surrender is not a weakness. It is the deepest expression of strength. It is saying: "I don't need to control everything to trust that I'm being carried."

Surrender makes space for guidance. And that guidance shows up as intuition, opportunity, protection, and peace. When you fight for control, you block your blessings. When you surrender, you allow them in.

5. The Code of Service

Every strong spirit eventually realizes this. You don't grow just for yourself. You grow so others can breathe easier because you exist.

Purpose becomes clearer when your life shifts from 'What do I need?' to 'Who can I lift?'. Service grounds you.

Service expands you. Service keeps your ego in check and your heart awake.

A spiritually aligned life is a life that leaves people better than you found them.

6. The Code of Gratitude

Gratitude is the final cheat code because it shifts your entire vibration.

You cannot be grateful and fearful at the same time. You cannot be grateful and bitter at the same time. You cannot be grateful and powerless at the same time.

Gratitude returns you to truth: You are already supported. You are already guided. You have already survived everything that tried to break you.

Gratitude turns survival into growth, and growth into grace.

If this entire book could be summarized in one sentence, it would be this:

Stay aligned with the voice inside you that refuses to fear life.

That voice is your advantage.

That voice is your protection.

That voice is your spiritual code.

When you live from that place, you are no longer reacting to life, you are led.

RESET POINT:

The Spiritual Alignment Reset

Take 10–12 minutes and write the following:

1. **Stillness:** What truth have you been avoiding that shows up when you get quiet?

2. **Trust:** Where in your life do you need to stop forcing and start trusting?

3. **Alignment:** What needs to shift for your life to feel more honest?

4. **Surrender:** What are you still trying to control that is costing you peace?

5. **Service:** Who can you uplift this week; genuinely, without expecting anything in return?

6. **Gratitude:** List five things you are grateful for right now that remind you that you're supported.

At some point in your life, you realize that growth isn't just a strategy, it is a calling. You can push, hustle, discipline, and force your way through decision after decision, but the real breakthroughs; the ones that shift your identity at the root, come from a place much deeper than effort. They come from alignment.

It knows who you are becoming.

It knows the path you keep sensing but haven't fully stepped into.

It knows the strength you doubt, the resilience you underestimate, the purpose you keep postponing.

And in this final chapter, I want you to hear this clearly:

You were never walking alone.

You've had access, all along to a *Source deeper* than fear, stronger than circumstance, and wiser than anything the world could ever tell you. You've had a connection that does not need perfect faith, only honest intention. You've had guidance that doesn't disappear when you feel lost; it simply waits for you to look inward again.

Spirituality is not about escaping the world. It is about moving through the world with a different centre. It's the moment you realize your power did not come from your achievements; it came from your alignment. It's the moment you understand that clarity isn't found in more information, it's found in listening.

It is the moment you finally accept that the life you're building isn't powered by will alone—it's supported by something greater. So, as you close this book, I want to leave you with this final truth: ***Your spirit already knows the way.***

Every next step you need is already inside you.

Every answer you've been looking for is already whispering.

Every breakthrough you're chasing is already unfolding.

Your only job now is to stay connected. Stay grounded. Stay open. And walk forward with the quiet confidence of someone who knows they are guided not by pressure, not by fear, not by expectation but by something wise, steady, and sacred.

If you let it, this connection will change everything.

Your life is no longer a search. It is becoming.

And you are ready.

THE PILLAR OF THE CHEAT CODE

This is not an ending. This is a handoff.

Everything you have read up to this point was designed to strip away the noise, the lies, the borrowed beliefs, and the identities you were never meant to wear. The Cheat Code was never about shortcuts, it was about clarity. And clarity rests on three pillars that cannot be negotiated, outsourced, or avoided.

Purpose.

Identity.

Ownership.

These are not concepts. They are laws.

Purpose

Purpose answers the question 'why you move?'.

Without purpose, effort feels heavy. Discipline feels forced. Motivation becomes a problem you're constantly trying to solve. Purpose removes friction. It gives direction to your energy and meaning to your pain.

Purpose is not found, it is decided.

When you decide why you are here, confusion loses its grip. Distractions become obvious. You stop chasing every opportunity and start building alignment. Purpose turns time into leverage.

Identity

Identity answers the question, 'who is moving?'.

You will never outperform the identity you secretly believe you are. Skills matter. Strategy matters. But identity always wins in the long run.

Change your habits without changing identity and you will relapse. Change your environment without changing identity and you will adapt back. Identity is the operating system. Everything else is an app.

When you upgrade how you see yourself, what you tolerate, what you expect, what you demand of yourself; your behaviour follows naturally. Identity removes the need for willpower.

Ownership

Ownership answers the question 'who is responsible?'.

This is where most people fail. Ownership means no excuses, no outsourcing blame, no waiting to be rescued. It means accepting full responsibility not just for your actions, but for your results.

Ownership is power. The moment you take ownership, you reclaim control.

■■■

FINAL THOUGHTS

This book was never meant to motivate you. Motivation fades. Comfort returns. Old patterns sneak back in.

This book was written to wake you up, to remind you that much of what you call your personality is conditioning. Much of what you call fear is borrowed thinking. Much of what you call your limits were installed without your permission. You were hypnotized slowly; by culture, by repetition, by expectations.

And page by page, idea by idea, this book was designed to de-hypnotize you.

Identity is not who they told you, you were. Purpose is not something you find; it is something you choose and own. And ownership is the moment you stop blaming, stop waiting, and stop asking for permission.

No one is coming to save you.

But the good news? You don't need saving.

You need awareness. You need courage. You need to tell the truth about the story you've been living and then rewrite it.

If this book made you uncomfortable, good.

Discomfort is the sound of conditioning breaking. If it challenges you, that's because growth does not whisper.

Now the work begins. Not tomorrow. Not when you're ready.

Now.

Live awake. Live deliberately. And never again give your mind to a system that profits from you staying asleep.

— Arnold

ABOUT THE AUTHOR

Arnold Best is a personal development coach and human behaviour strategist with over a decade of experience transforming lives across the world. As a certified NLP practitioner, body language expert, and specialist in human behaviour, Arnold has built a reputation for decoding what drives people, and helping them create rapid, lasting change.

He is the creator and host of The Lab Radio, the Caribbean's first and only personal development radio station, where he delivers daily strategies for mental mastery, emotional intelligence, and peak performance. Arnold is also a dynamic keynote speaker, workshop facilitator, and interventionist who has trained professionals, executives, and organizations in personal leadership and behavioural change.

His professional journey includes working alongside and learning directly from global leaders in the field of transformation, Dr Paul Eckman, Mr Tony Robbins, and Dr Wayne Dyer. Also, serving as part of Tony Robbins' crew and completing the renowned 'firewalk' experience five times. These experiences strengthened his command of state management, physiology, communication patterns, and the psychology of breakthrough.

Arnold's expertise spans micro-expressions, nonverbal

communication, decision psychology, emotional mastery, strategic intervention, and identity transformation. His work blends neuroscience, behavioural science, coaching, and NLP into a results-driven system that has helped thousands gain clarity, overcome limiting beliefs, and elevate their life trajectory.

With a proven track record, a decade of hands-on experience, and a commitment to excellence, Arnold Best stands as one of the Caribbean's leading voices in personal development, performance psychology, and human transformation.

Made in the USA
Coppell, TX
11 June 2026

81087291R00089